School Liturgies
Made Easy

School Liturgies Made Easy

Lisa Freemantle and Carmela Caporiccio

NOVALIS

© 2012 Novalis Publishing Inc.

Cover: Blaine Herrmann
Layout: Audrey Wells
Interior images: Eugene Kral, except for page 53 (Caroline Gagnon)

Published by Novalis

Publishing Office
10 Lower Spadina Avenue, Suite 400
Toronto, Ontario, Canada
M5V 2Z2

Head Office
4475 Frontenac Street
Montréal, Québec, Canada
H2H 2S2

www.novalis.ca

Library and Archives Canada Cataloguing in Publication

Freemantle, Lisa, 1962-
        School liturgies made easy / Lisa Freemantle and Carmela Caporiccio.

Includes bibliographical references.

ISBN 978-2-89646-408-1

    1. Catholic Church--Liturgy. 2. Catholic Church--
Education. 3. Children's liturgies. 4. Worship (Religious
education). I. Caporiccio, Carmela II. Title.

BX2045.C553F74 2012   264'.0203083   C2012-903645-5

Printed in Canada.

We acknowledge the financial support of the Government of Canada through the Canada Book Fund for business development activities.

5 4 3 2 1   16   15   14   13   12

Contents

With grateful hearts, we would like to acknowledge all those who helped in the creation of this resource, especially our families, our colleagues in the York Catholic District School Board, as well as Joe Sinasac, Grace Deutsch and Anne Louise Mahoney at Novalis.

May they always be guided by the gentle hand of God.

Introduction

School Liturgies Made Easy is a step-by-step guide that helps you prepare a Mass or prayer service for elementary school students. This manual offers everything you need as you begin your preparations, including what happens during each part of the Mass, how to find readings, who reads what, how to select music, how to involve students, and much more.

For both of us, attending Sunday Mass is a regular part of life, and has been for as long as we can remember. Because we attended Catholic schools, Masses and prayer services were part of our education. Eventually, when we grew up, we each got married. Our kids also went to Mass every Sunday and attended Catholic schools. As teachers in the Catholic school system, we signed up to prepare Masses and prayer services for the school. How hard could it be? we thought. After all, we'd been to countless Masses and prayer services! And then we thought… "Help! Where do we begin?"

Does this sound familiar? It wasn't until we had to prepare our first school Mass that we realized how little we actually knew about the whole process. Over time, we gained experience, learning a lot through trial and error. Along the way, we asked questions, read books, collaborated with other teaching peers, talked to our parish priests and attended workshops.

Once we had collected all this helpful information, it occurred to us that a manual that led teachers through the process step by step would have been very helpful in our early years of teaching.

Many of our colleagues felt the same way. The result is *School Liturgies Made Easy*. It is our hope that it helps you create many beautiful and prayerful services and Masses for your students.

Blessings,
Carmela and **Lisa**

1

Why We Prepare and Celebrate Liturgies with Our Students

As teachers and students, we celebrate together for both educational and liturgical reasons. Let's look at each reason individually.

Educational Rationale

Today's students are exposed to many secular influences. As Catholic educators, we work with the Church and the home to instill in students a love for and trust in God, along with a fervent wish to honour our rich faith traditions. For Catholic school students, prayer is so important to their development as Christians that it is a key part of school life and the curriculum.

As educators, we pray with our students for many reasons:

- To meet certain curriculum expectations, we teach students the Church's traditional prayers, such as the Our Father, the Creed and the Rosary.

- As a Christian community, we pray together to ask God for forgiveness, to praise God, to celebrate God's gifts, and to thank God for our many blessings.

- To facilitate the encounter with Jesus.

- To meet God in the sacraments, we celebrate the Eucharist and the sacrament of Reconciliation. (We may also help the parish to prepare students for First Communion, Reconciliation and Confirmation.)

- To mark the seasons of the Church year, we celebrate such key times as Advent, Christmas, Ash Wednesday, Lent, Holy Week, the Easter season, and Ordinary Time.

- To mark significant moments in the life of our school, such as school events, transitions in students' lives, funerals, the start and end of the school year, and graduation.

- Like the wider community around us, we celebrate secular events such as Thanksgiving and Remembrance Day, but in Catholic schools we make connections to God's role in them.

- To honour our school's patron saint, we pray together on his or her feast day.

All these forms of prayer and celebration have something in common: through them, in a meaningful way, we share with and pass on to our students our rich Catholic faith and traditions. As Catholic educators, we are called to help our students grow up confident and happy in the knowledge of their faith and

God's love for them, so that it may nourish them and they may in turn pass it on to future generations.

Liturgical Reasons

For many of our students, their most regular experience of liturgy happens at school, so it is vital that we "get it right"! Getting it right means providing liturgically sound yet age-appropriate celebrations.

To some teachers, such a task seems to be filled with insurmountable difficulties. They overplan, and celebrations can feel forced or joyless. Others view liturgical celebrations as just another assembly, and the result is an unsatisfying time filler. But there is a happy medium.

To "get it right," teachers need to follow these four major guidelines:

- be organized,
- have a clear purpose,
- encourage wide participation, and
- ensure that your celebration is liturgically sound.

Be organized

Being organized means that students know exactly what is expected of them. Their roles should be clearly defined and spelled out. Each student in the group should feel they have contributed something by helping to prepare the celebration in some way, taking on a specific role during the celebration, or participating as a member of the assembly.

Have a clear purpose

Students should understand, at their own level, what they are praying for and why. Our main purpose for celebrating with students is to help them to pray and to praise God well. This always involves the environment, the Scriptures and music chosen, and the way we prepare the students to be a "consciously participating" assembly (*Constitution on the Sacred Liturgy*, #14). We highlight this participation differently through the liturgical year: Advent, Christmas, Lent, Easter and Ordinary Time.

Encourage wide participation

Make every effort to include your students in the preparations for and the celebration of every liturgy. Students of all levels and age groups can contribute. Make sure they feel comfortable, prepared and welcomed.

Ensure that your celebration is liturgically sound

As you prepare, make sure your celebration respects liturgical norms and practices. Students will absorb these over time as they discover that communal liturgy is much more than saying nice words. Through your example, they will learn to treat the Word of God and the Eucharist with respect and will be formed in good liturgical practices.

Walking with Students on Their Faith Journeys

As teachers, we have a major influence in the lives of our students. After all, for ten months of the year they spend many of their waking hours in our company. They watch us. They listen to us. They emulate us. They ask us countless questions. They want to know how they fit into the faith picture. That's why we need to model what we'd like to see in our students. It's a big job, but as trained Catholic educators, we are up for the challenge.

Every student will be in a different place in their understanding of their faith. Some students are just beginning to explore their beliefs. Some are already well on their way. And some are in between. You are also travelling along your own faith path. None of us travels in exactly the same way or at exactly the same rate. All of us have our own doubts, concerns and questions. But we know that God is always present, listening to our prayers, loving us abundantly and offering understanding and guidance. By providing a rich liturgical environment for our students, we help them to flourish and grow as they travel on their faith journeys.

Notes

2

Collaborating with the Parish Priest

Whenever you celebrate a Mass or prayer service as a school community, you will work in close partnership with the parish priest who is connected to your school. Arrange to meet with him to plan your liturgies. Before your meeting, prepare a list of questions to ask. This will help you to keep track of your queries and his answers.

What to Ask

Your questions will fall under two broad categories: liturgical and logistical. Most school prayer services happen on the school premises; if you want the priest to lead a prayer service, most of your queries will be liturgical ones. You will also want to discuss scheduling and timing of the celebration. If you are planning a Mass with your students at the church or school, then your inquiries will be both logistical and liturgical ones, as the Mass follows specific liturgical norms.

Liturgical Questions

These questions will be about two main areas: readings and prayers, and music.

Readings and Prayers

1. *For Masses*, you will usually use the readings of the Mass of the day. (These are approved by the Canadian bishops for use in Canada. However, you can ask your priest for permission to choose different biblical readings for your celebration, if the prescribed readings are too difficult or are not appropriate for your students, for example. You may *not* use non-biblical readings.) You will find that most priests allow these changes, especially for younger students. They understand that because a school celebration involves much more student participation, it differs from a parish Mass.

You will need to choose a First Reading and a Gospel. (See *Chapter 10* for information on how to select readings.) You will also need to prepare the Prayer of the Faithful. (See *Chapter 6* for how to write these prayers of intercession.) If the priest agrees, you may write the opening or concluding prayers for the Mass, but this tends to be the exception. For more information about Masses, including adapting the language of the presidential (priest's) prayers, consult the *Directory for Masses with Children*. (See *Appendix 3*.)

2. *For prayer services*, you will select readings from the New or Old Testaments. Usually only one reading is required. If the priest will preside, ask him to approve the other prayers you will include. Many available resources offer ready-made prayer services you can use. (See *Appendix 3*.)

For Masses and prayer services, make sure that all the readings and prayers you select are suitable for the age of the students – both for the readers and for those who will be listening.

Music

1. It is always preferable for Masses with children to have live music and instrumentation. In schools where musicians or music leaders are lacking, you may need to play recorded instrumental music or sing along with a hymn on a CD or mp3 player. Whether you use live or recorded music for Masses or prayer services with young children, choose simpler hymns or songs with refrains to encourage wide participation; you will find that most priests are open to these song choices as long as they are appropriate for the liturgy. (See *Chapter 10* for more on Music Selection.)

Logistical Questions

Logistical questions fall into three main groups: scheduling, equipment, and key locations. For both Masses and prayer services, scheduling with your priest is very important. Most of the questions below refer to celebrating a Mass in the church, as teachers tend to know the logistics in their school.

Scheduling

Some priests are responsible for more than one school community. Because they also have many parish duties, they have very busy schedules. That is why scheduling and timing issues are so important when you are preparing a liturgical celebration that will involve the parish priest.

1. Many schools celebrate Masses or prayer services for the following times and events: Thanksgiving, Remembrance Day, Advent, Epiphany, Ash Wednesday, Lent, Holy Week, Easter, Reconciliation, First Communion and Confirmation. At the beginning of the school year, decide which of these (or any additional ones) your school plans to celebrate with the priest and then schedule these with him well in advance.

2. If you will celebrate Mass in the parish church, make sure to book the church for the celebration and for the rehearsal. (It is best to do a run-through of your celebration, including entry and exit, sitting, kneeling and standing, reading and singing, the sign of peace, going to communion and returning to seats.) This is especially important for younger students, but all age groups will benefit from rehearsal on location.

Equipment

1. Many churches have built-in sound systems that are switched on at a central location. Ask the priest or parish secretary for permission to use it. Find out where it is and if keys are required to access the controls. Ask for a demonstration on how to use it properly and adjust the volume, if needed. Finally, make sure you know where and how to put everything away when you are finished with it.

2. For young readers and cantors, a stool or riser may be available for easier access to the microphones. Ask if you can use it, or bring your own.

3. If you will have live music, ask about microphones and their stands, music stands and permission to use church instruments (organ or piano). If lyrics will be projected on overheads or PowerPoint slides, find out where the electrical outlets are and investigate where to place the screen and the overhead projector or laptop. If you will need a CD player or mp3 speakers, check on where you can plug these in. Will you need extension cords? Find out if any of this equipment is available for your use or if you need to provide your own. Test all equipment ahead of time and on the day of the celebration to avoid technical glitches.

Key locations

1. Find out where the bathrooms are. Although you will no doubt take your students to the bathroom before coming to the church, some of your younger charges may still need to use the bathroom when they arrive or during Mass.

2. Ask the priest where and when the altar servers should meet him before Mass begins. If they are to be vested, ask where the albs will be.

3. Ask the priest for permission to arrive early on the day of the Mass to set up equipment, arrange readers and musicians, and settle the other students. Make sure the church will be open when you get there.

Always give the priest a complete copy of the readings, prayers and music you have chosen well in advance so he can review them. If changes need to be made, you will then have ample time to choose alternative ones and prepare your students.

Parish priests know that students (especially primary students) need a lot of time and effort to practise and prepare readings, songs and rituals. Like you, priests want community prayer to be a positive and faith-filled experience for all. They will gladly work with you and will help guide you along the way. So be patient, be flexible, be organized and be prepared.

Notes

3

The Liturgical Calendar

Like any calendar, the liturgical calendar highlights certain seasons and special days. Each season or feast of the liturgical year is a key part of our faith tradition. The liturgical year contains a number of seasons:

- Advent
- Christmas
- Ordinary Time
- Lent
- Easter.

When preparing a Mass or prayer service, you must know which liturgical season you will be in at the time of the celebration. There are several things to keep in mind:

- make sure the environment and decor match the season's colour and use appropriate symbols;
- if it is Lent, avoid saying or singing the word "Alleluia" in your song choices, prayers and readings;
- if it is a special feast day, think about what you need to include.

Check a liturgical calendar (available as a book or online) for details on the Church year. We will explore each season briefly below. The Ordo or Liturgical Calendar is published annually by the National Liturgy Office of the Canadian Conference of Catholic Bishops.

Advent

The Church year begins on the First Sunday of Advent – the Sunday closest to November 30. (Advent can therefore start as early as November 27 or as late as December 3.) Advent continues until December 24. This joyful season of waiting is dedicated to preparing our hearts for the birth of Christ. The first two weeks of the Advent season focus on the heavenly feast at the end of time, and the last two weeks focus on remembering and celebrating Jesus' birth as one of us.

Part of our preparation involves self-examination and confession (penitence), when we admit that our lives and our world are not as God intended them to be. The liturgical colour for this season is a royal purple, which, although penitential, is not meant to be the same here as used in the penitential season of Lent.

There are four candles in the Advent wreath, one for each week. Three are purple and one is pink. The pink candle is lit on Gaudete (Rejoice) Sunday – the Third Sunday of Advent – as a signal to rejoice because the waiting is almost over.

Christmas

The word "Christmas" means the "Mass" (or celebration) of Christ. This season begins with the feast of Christmas on December 25.

During this season, the Church focuses on the birth of Jesus. January 6 is the feast of the Epiphany. "Epiphany" means "to show" or "to shine upon." Jesus' majesty was revealed to the three kings, who represented all the nations of the world. His light of purity and truth shines upon us all. The season of Christmas usually lasts until the Baptism of Jesus, which means that often the first week back to school after the holidays is still Christmas season. The liturgical colour for Christmas is white.

Ordinary Time

Ordinary Time is the weeks between Epiphany and Ash Wednesday, and the weeks between Pentecost and the First Sunday of Advent. It is called "ordinary" not because it is not special, but because these weeks are numbered or "ordered" throughout the year (this comes from the Latin word *ordinalis*).

The part of Ordinary Time between Epiphany and Ash Wednesday may have as few as four Sundays or as many as nine, depending on the date of Easter, which changes from year to year. During this part of Ordinary Time, we hear about Jesus beginning his earthly ministry. In the Mass readings we hear of his first miracle at the wedding of Cana, when he changed the water into wine. We also hear how he called his disciples. It is a time of growth as he spreads the Good News of God's love for all people. The liturgical colour for this season is green.

Lent

The word "Lent" has two sources: Latin (*quadragesima*, or "40"), and Anglo-Saxon, meaning "spring," when the days lengthened. Throughout this season, we reflect on Jesus' dying on the cross for us. During Lent, we do not sing or say "Alleluia," but wait for his

resurrection at Easter before proclaiming this word of joy. Lent begins on Ash Wednesday. It ends on Holy Thursday, when we begin the three-day Paschal Triduum, which takes us to Easter and the resurrection. Lent lasts for 40 days (this doesn't include Sundays). This is a time of penitence, so the liturgical colour is purple.

During Lent, we are asked especially to pray, to fast and to give alms.

• Prayer

Prayer is a focus during Lent as we remember Jesus' great sacrifice for us. (All through Lent, try to make a special effort to pray regularly with your students. A short daily prayer or simple phrase works well with younger students. Older students may want to write prayers of their own to share.)

• Fasting

We fast or abstain from eating certain foods during Lent. Many Catholics do not eat meat on Friday, for example. Some adult Catholics fast all day or for part of the day on certain days, such as Ash Wednesday and Good Friday. We can also "fast" from negative behaviours, such as selfishness or being critical. Younger students could be encouraged to do something for others, such as make their bed without being asked, or clear away their dishes after a meal. Older students could be invited to avoid name-calling or judging others.

• Almsgiving

Giving alms means sharing what we have with those who have less, or giving to the poor. This can be money, food, time or anything we have to share. During Lent, encourage your students to look out for and help those in need in their community however they can. For example, they could invite a student who is alone to play with them at recess, or phone their grandparents to say "I love you."

Holy Week begins with Passion (Palm) Sunday, when we remember Jesus' triumphant entry into Jerusalem. It concludes with the Triduum, which is a single celebration that lasts for three days (counted from sundown to sundown). On day 1 of the Triduum, we celebrate the Mass of the Lord's Supper (on Holy Thursday) and the veneration of the cross (on Good Friday). The focus of Good Friday is not the crucifixion so much as happily venerating the cross by which our salvation was won. Then the church is silent during day 2 (sundown Friday to sundown Saturday). At the beginning of day 3, in the darkness of the Easter morning (after the sun has set), the Church celebrates the mother of all liturgies: the Easter Vigil. The Triduum ends later that day at sundown on Sunday. If your students attend Mass with their families on Holy Thursday, they will witness the ritual of the washing of the feet, commemorating that Jesus washed the feet of his disciples at the Last Supper to model service for them. On this day, we remember that Jesus gave himself to us in the first Eucharist, and hear of

his subsequent arrest that same day. On Good Friday we focus on the suffering, crucifixion and death of our Saviour. The Easter Vigil leads us through the key stories of our faith and celebrates the wonder of the resurrection.

During Holy Week, you may want to pray the Stations of the Cross as a class or as a school. Although this devotion can be prayed at any time, it is especially poignant during Holy Week, since the Stations describe the final hours of Jesus' life. Many fine resources (print and online) are available to help you to prepare the Stations.

Easter

The season of Easter begins with the Easter Vigil and ends 50 days later, on the feast of Pentecost. Easter is the high point of the liturgical year and the most important season of the Christian calendar, when we rejoice that Jesus Christ has risen in majesty! During this time, the Mass readings celebrate the beginning of the Church, the coming of the Holy Spirit, appearances of the risen Lord, the forgiveness of sins and the promise of everlasting life.

At Easter, we leave behind the dark, penitential days of Lent, feasting as we begin anew in the light of the Risen Lord. We can again say and sing "Alleluia" with great joy! We are said to be an Easter people because we celebrate the resurrection and ascension of Jesus in our lives. In your classroom, have students decorate the word "Alleluia" on colourful paper and display their creations for all to enjoy.

The Easter season contains six Sundays. The liturgical colour of this season is white. During this time, share the resurrection stories with your students or have them draw or act out the stories.

Pentecost marks the joyous end to the Easter season. On this Sunday, we remember Jesus sending his disciples out into the world to spread the Good News. At Pentecost, the disciples found themselves speaking the languages of other lands by the power of the Holy Spirit. The liturgical colour for Pentecost, red, represents the flames of the Holy Spirit that descended on the first Pentecost.

Ordinary Time

Ordinary Time begins again after Pentecost and ends on the First Sunday of Advent. (Although there is only one season of Ordinary Time in the liturgical year, this season is split into two parts.) Ordinary Time is the longest season of the Church year.

Here we focus on Jesus' earthly ministry and teachings, and our mission as Christ's disciples. We are Christ's hands and feet, carrying on his work in the world. We dedicate ourselves to learning and practising how to live out our Christian faith. Together, with God's love to guide us, we make the kingdom of God grow. The liturgical colour for this season is green.

At Mass, we hear stories of Jesus' miracles, such as feeding thousands of people in the wilderness with a few loaves of bread and two fish, and bringing back to life a child who has died. We also hear his stories about the kingdom of God.

The Cycle of Liturgical Years

The Gospels contain the words and deeds of Christ according to the four evangelists: Matthew, Mark, Luke and John. These four New Testament books describe events in the life of Jesus. Written for different audiences and at various times after Jesus' death and resurrection, they portray similar events from different points of view.

It would be impossible to read all the Gospels in their entirety over the course of a year at Sunday Mass. To present the Gospels more fully, they have been divided into three liturgical years. In Year A, we hear the Gospel according to Matthew; in Year B, we listen to the Gospel according to Mark and chapter 6 of the Gospel of John; and in Year C, the Gospel of Luke is proclaimed. The Gospel of John does not have its own "year"; instead, it is proclaimed during Easter and at other times in each year of the cycle.

The three-year liturgical cycle (Years A, B and C) applies to all Sunday Masses. Weekday Masses follow a two-year cycle: Year I and Year II.

When preparing a Mass, make sure you know the liturgical year you are in so you can find the right readings. This information is found in the Ordo and on the website of the Canadian Conference of Catholic Bishops. It can also be found at the beginning of weekly missalettes and Sunday missals. Since most school Masses are on weekdays, you will usually check the readings for weekdays (Year I or Year II) first.

Environment and Decor

At Sunday Mass, you will notice that the colour of the priest's vestments and possibly the wall hangings change with the liturgical seasons. (The altar cloth is always white.)

If you celebrate school Masses at the parish church, you will not need to decorate for the season. For Masses and prayer services that will be held at the school, you will need to decorate according to the liturgical season. Here are some general guidelines.

Guidelines for Decoration

Certain items may be used to decorate your prayer space no matter what the season or occasion. These include unscented candles (in off-white or the correct liturgical colour), a crucifix and a Bible. Other items will depend on the liturgical season. The table below lists the liturgical colour(s) for each season along with symbols you could use for these times. None of these items should be placed on the altar or obscure the altar.

Season/Celebration	Liturgical Colour	Symbols or Signs
Advent	royal purple	Advent wreath, Jesse Tree
Third Sunday of Advent (Gaudete Sunday)	rose (pink)	Advent wreath (two purple candles and the pink one are lit)
Christmas	white	crèche
Ordinary Time	green	flowers
Lent Fourth Sunday in Lent	purple rose (pink)	ashes, stones or pebbles, cactus plants, cross draped in purple or sackcloth
Easter	white	dove, lilies, coloured eggs, bare cross with white linen draped on it, clear glass bowl filled with water
Triduum	Holy Thursday: white Good Friday: red Holy Saturday (daytime): purple Easter Vigil and Easter Sunday: white	bowl of water (washing of the feet), bread and wine (Last Supper), cross, crown of thorns, Stations of the Cross
Reconciliation	purple (if during Advent or Lent)	sand or stones (Jesus tempted in the desert)
Confirmation and Pentecost	red	dove, fire symbols (Holy Spirit)
First Communion	white	dove, signs of peace, flowers, lamb
Funerals All Souls' Day (November 1)	white	cross, pictures or photographs of the person who has died

Notes

4

Should You Have a Mass or a Prayer Service?

The Catholic Church has three official liturgical services: the Mass; the Liturgy of the Word (the first half of the Mass, which follows a particular format); and the Liturgy of the Hours (Morning and Evening Prayer). Schools often celebrate another, unofficial type of service: the prayer service.

Prayer, whether in a formal setting such as Mass or a more informal one such as a prayer service, opens the door to group praise and thanksgiving, forgiveness and hope, sharing and outreach. Encourage your students to engage in the liturgy.

This chapter will help you decide whether a Mass or a prayer service is more appropriate for your celebration.

At Mass, We Celebrate a Sacrament

Celebrating Mass as a school is a special opportunity for the community to gather for the Eucharist. All are welcome; people arrive and greet each other. As at most celebrations, those gathered do not merely attend and watch, as they would a show; instead, they are called upon to participate and immerse themselves in the celebration with joy.

The environment in the church reflects the liturgical season. The Mass follows a particular order: we gather as a community; we listen to God's Word; we give thanks; we share in the

body and blood of Christ. As we leave, we are commissioned or sent to share with others the Good News of God's love for all people.

Prayer Services Allow for Flexibility

Prayer services also gather the community. All are welcomed upon arrival. The environment and decor also reflect the liturgical season. Those gathered are called upon to take part in various ways, including (though not limited to) spoken responses, gestures, dance, listening, song, drama, prayer and movement. Unlike Masses, prayer services do not follow a prescribed order and there is no Eucharist. Prayer services are open invitations to prayer that can be structured or informal. They allow flexibility in format and length, and are versatile, as they can be celebrated anywhere and anytime. They do not require the presence of a priest.

Mass or Prayer Service?

So how do you decide whether a Mass or prayer service is best for your celebration? Here are a few things to think about.

- *How much time do you have to prepare?* Masses require more time and planning.

- *What can your students handle?* Consider the shorter attention span of younger students.

- *How easy is it to take students to the church?* Certain times of year may be better than others for this trek.

- *When can the gymnasium be available for the preparation and celebration of Mass?*

- *Are the church and the parish priest available?* Think about where the celebration could be held.

- *What is the purpose of your prayer?* Highlighting the liturgical year, such as Advent, Lent or Easter, or honouring the feast day of your school's patron saint, might best be celebrated with Mass. A secular event such as Remembrance Day is better suited to a prayer service.

Younger students are usually just beginning to pray with the larger community. They are excited to learn about their loving God. Try to engage them in praying at their level to fuel that excitement. Primary students may not be able to proclaim readings, but they can be involved in the liturgy in other meaningful ways. For example, they can join in group responses or lead simple repetitive prayers. They can sing with all of the assembly or can be in a procession. In a prayer service, students might prepare a simple drama of a Scripture story.

Be sure to involve older students as well. Some might be reserved in their expression of faith, internalizing what they believe; they may seem blasé or unimpressed on the outside. This is not to say they are not faithful; they may simply not be comfortable in expressing openly what they believe. Others may be willing to participate. Still others may surprise you with the depth of their faith.

Whether you choose a Mass or a prayer service, invite students to participate "fully, consciously and actively" in praising God, as the *Constitution on the Sacred Liturgy* says (#14).

Chapter 5 describes how to prepare a prayer service. *Chapter 6* explores how to prepare a Mass.

5

Preparing a Prayer Service

In this chapter, we will talk about the nuts and bolts of preparing a prayer service. If you choose to prepare your own, this chapter will help you to decide what to put in it and how to go about it. If you plan to use an existing prayer service (see *Appendix 3*), you will find some explanations and descriptions about what to look for and how to create a meaningful experience for all involved.

Choosing an Appropriate Title

Whether you are preparing your own prayer service or using one that you have found, make sure the title reflects the theme of your prayer. For instance, if you are having a Lenten prayer service and have taken the service from a book that contains several Lenten services, make sure the title is descriptive (and not just "Lent 1," for example). If your focus is on sacrifice, then *Lent: Sacrifice* would do, but a more evocative title might be *Lent: Through the Desert*. A strong title ensures that those gathered understand why you are praying. Younger students especially may relate better to a concrete image of a desert rather than an abstract concept such as sacrifice. A good title also serves as a useful organizational tool when you eventually file the prayer service for future reference (see *Chapter 12*).

Call to Worship

The Call to Worship for a prayer service is typically very brief. Decide who will read the introduction – usually it is an adult or older student. Welcome all who have gathered for the prayer service. You may begin with the sign of the cross, so that your prayer is in the name of God the Father, the Son and the Holy Spirit. If you have any special intentions, you may wish to add them here. Finally, if there is to be an opening hymn or song, conclude your introduction by announcing it.

A sample introduction for an Easter prayer service follows.

Today we welcome all of you with joy as we come together this Easter to celebrate Jesus, the Lord, who has been raised to new life. We praise our God and we rejoice in his new life, which he shares with all people.

Let us begin our prayer service by making the sign of the cross. In the name of the Father…

Let us now join in singing our opening song,

Opening Prayer

A greeting and an opening prayer usually follow the opening song. Make sure the prayer starts by calling on God (e.g., God of Power,

God of All, God of Love) and is made through his Son, Jesus Christ. The Opening Prayer is usually done by an adult or older student.

A sample opening prayer for Lent follows:

Gracious God,

Teach us how to live in peace during this Lenten season. Help us to receive your love in our lives. May your love grow within us, so that our lives mirror the love you have for your people. We make this prayer to you through your Son, Jesus Christ, who is the Prince of Peace forever and ever.

All: **Amen.**

Offerings or Symbols

One option is to "set" the environment for prayer. Select symbol bearers and a reader. You may wish to include symbols that will remind the assembly of the reason for gathering. While these can be brought up at any time, it is often best to bring them up early in the prayer service, since these symbols can set the environment, draw the eye to your prayer focal point, and highlight the theme of the prayer service. Carrying them in during the opening hymn is one option; in this case you would not include the explanations, to avoid interrupting the liturgy once it has begun.

A variety of items can be brought up at this time. The symbols chosen should reflect the liturgical season. Other symbols could highlight the Scripture and prayer. Although students of any age can bring gifts to the prayer focal point, this is a great opportunity to engage younger students who may not be comfortable with other roles.

As each item is placed on or near the prayer focus table, have a reader identify the symbol and briefly explain why it has been brought there. If these explanations are simple enough, they can be read by primary students.

Some sample explanations for symbols of the beginning of the school year follow:

1. *We bring a bible to remember the faith that we share.*
2. *We bring books as symbols of our always learning new things.*
3. *We bring this tambourine to remind us of the songs we sing in praise of God.*
4. *We bring these flowers to remind us of our friendships that will blossom with God's love.*
5. *We bring a globe to remind us that no matter where we are, we must continue to reach out to others to share our love and faith.*

Bringing symbols up is optional. You may instead have everything in place as part of the environment before the celebration begins.

Scripture Reading

Every prayer service should be rooted in the Word of God. To this end, select an appropriate reading for the theme you have chosen. (Be sure to introduce the reading by stating the name of the book – e.g., if the reading is from 1 Corinthians, begin with "A reading from the first Letter of Saint Paul to the Corinthians." We do not proclaim the chapter and verse numbers.) If you are writing your own prayer service, many books are available to help you select the readings. (See *Chapter 10* and *Appendix 3*). These books list topics alphabetically and then list readings that deal with each topic. Make sure the reading you have chosen is age appropriate for your students. Select a strong reader to proclaim the reading.

Prayer of the Faithful

These prayers are optional in a prayer service, but they are usually part of a Mass. If you decide to include them, you will need to follow some general guidelines.

The prayers of petition should be short, simple and to the point. Each one should be no more than one sentence long. There are usually four to six of these prayers. They can be read by one reader or several. If the wording is simple enough, primary students can read them.

1. Your first prayer should be for the needs of the Church. This can include the priest, the Pope, the bishops or all members of the Church.
2. The second prayer is for public authorities, including political figures.
3. The third prayer is usually for those who are suffering or in need, such as those who have been affected by natural disasters, conflicts or war. Here you can include the sick and those who care for them, the poor and the marginalized of society.
4. The fourth prayer is for the local community and should include all those gathered for your prayer service, and/or something happening within your community (e.g., "For all who are celebrating their First Communion during the Easter season").
5. Any special intentions or prayers for those who have died can be added at the end.

Choose or write a simple response for the assembly to say after each prayer, such as "Lord, hear our prayer." Or teach students a sung response with gestures, such as the one used in the Born of the Spirit Catechetical Program from the Canadian Conference of Catholic Bishops.

Here are some sample intercessions for the First Week of Advent.

*The response is: "**Lord, hear our prayer.**"*

1. *For the Pope, _____, our bishop, _____, and our parish priest, _____, as they share faith and hope with others this Advent. We pray OR We pray to the Lord. **R.***

2. *For the nations of the world, called to live in hope and love. We pray OR We pray to the Lord. **R.***

3. *For those who are lonely this Advent, in need of the joy and hope of the coming birth of Christ. We pray OR We pray to the Lord. **R.***

4. *For those who are sick this Advent and longing to be filled with hope and to feel the healing grace of God. We pray OR We pray to the Lord. **R.***

5. *For all of us here as we wait in hope as Mary did for the birth of Jesus. We pray OR We pray to the Lord. **R.***

6. *For all the people in our province whose lives have been affected by the fire over the weekend, who have a special need for hope, faith, love and joy this Advent season. We pray OR We pray to the Lord. **R.***

The presider always invites the gathered assembly to pray the Prayer of the Faithful. For example: "Certain of God's care, we pray for the Church and the world."

Similarly, the presider always concludes the Prayer of the Faithful. For example:

"Generous God, you lavish your bounty on your people. Hear the prayers that we ask in the name of Jesus Christ, our Lord."

Litanies, Group Reflections, Rituals and Liturgical Dance

Litanies, group reflections, rituals and liturgical dance are listed as optional in the Planning Guide for Prayer Services. (See *Appendix 1*.) These activities can enrich the prayer and reflection of the gathered assembly, especially when there is no homily. It is best to use only one of these options, to avoid overloading the prayer. Which one you choose will depend on your comfort level and the dynamics of the group. Usually these "activities" are a response to the Scripture proclaimed.

For titles of books containing prayer services that include Litanies, Reflections, Rituals and Liturgical Dance, see *Appendix 3*.

Let's look at each one briefly.

Litanies

Some prayer services include a litany, which is a form of communal prayer with a response.

The structure of these prayers can vary. To promote wide participation, use a structure similar to the Prayer of the Faithful. Or divide the group into two groups (left side and right side). Or select a number of readers to read the different parts.

One beautiful litany is the Litany of Saints, which tends to be recited or sung communally on All Saints' Day and at the Easter Vigil, but can be used throughout the year. The Litany of the Saints is led by one person or by the choir, with the people saying or singing the response ("Pray for us") after each line.

For primary students, litanies made up of simple phrases that follow a predictable pattern work well. Dividing the group into two, with one group leading and one group answering, promotes group cohesiveness and ensures wide involvement.

A litany of thanksgiving is often a suitable response, especially for primary children. Here are two examples for a Thanksgiving prayer service:

Leader: For fruits and vegetables and all the gifts of the harvest.
All: We give you thanks, O God.

Leader: For the beauty of this season in the trees and the leaves.
All: We give you thanks, O God.

Singing the communal response with an accompanying gesture is a wonderful way to encourage participation and embody the prayer.

Reflections

For older students, you may wish to include a time for silent reflection. Typically, the leader asks a number of guided, open-ended questions and then allows the group to contemplate these questions silently for a few minutes. Questions should be thought-provoking but are not meant to lead to discussion during the prayer service. The time given for the reflection should be long enough to allow students to think about each question, but short enough that students don't become restless. For primary students, one or two questions and a minute of silent reflection is plenty. For older students, three or four questions and two to three minutes of reflection is fine. Adjust the timing according to the needs of the group.

Ritual Gestures

Rituals are simple, shared actions by a representative group or the entire assembly. Both primary and junior students can take part. These can include such actions as sharing the sign of peace, placing symbolic objects, or doing a simple group movement, such as a procession. Ritual gestures must be done prayerfully and solemnly if they are to be meaningful. Each prayer service will lend itself to different types of ritual gestures. (See *Appendix 3.*)

Liturgical Dance

If a staff member has led liturgical dance or danced in a liturgical celebration before, this form of dance can be a wonderful addition to any prayer service and works well for all ages. These dances are another way of praying – you can use banners or flowing robes, or keep things more simple. A number of excellent resources explain basic movements that can be taught to large and small groups. Liturgical dance should add to the prayer experience rather than distract from it; the dancers should be dressed appropriately for a liturgical setting. (See *Appendix 3.*)

Closing Prayer

The prayer service concludes with a closing prayer. (Any announcements, such as how to exit the space, are made before the closing prayer.) This prayer is generally read by an adult or older student. It begins by addressing God (e.g., God our Father, God of Compassion and Goodness, Gracious God) and continues with words of thanks or praise. We always make our prayers to God through his Son, Jesus Christ. We end the prayer with "Amen." At the very end of the prayer service, it is an option to make the sign of the cross. After the Closing Prayer, announce the closing song, if there is one.

A sample Closing Prayer for Thanksgiving follows.

God our Father,

We thank you for the opportunity to learn, to develop friendships and to grow in body and in faith this year. Help us to appreciate these gracious gifts and use them in your service. We ask this through your Son, Jesus Christ, our Lord.

All: **Amen**.

Our closing song is:

_____

As you plan, consult the Prayer Service Planning Guide and the Prayer Service Summary Sheet (see *Appendix 1*). These easy-to-use worksheets will lead you step by step through your planning. Once you have completed your planning on the itemized Prayer Service Planning Guide, use the Summary Sheet as a quick reference tool. These worksheets can easily be stored for future use. (See *Chapter 12.*)

Notes

6

Preparing a Mass

To participate fully in the celebration of Mass, everyone needs to know their part: when to sit and when to stand, when to process and when to kneel, when to speak and what to say, when to sing, when to listen, and when to pray. In this chapter, we will review the parts of the Mass. We will explain which parts belong to the assembly and which to the priest.

The Mass is made up of four main parts: the Introductory Rites, the Liturgy of the Word, the Liturgy of the Eucharist, and the Concluding Rites. We will look at each one in turn.

We recommend that you consult the *Directory for Masses with Children*, from the Vatican Congregation for Divine Worship, when planning school Masses. It is available online and offers guidance on the readings, prayers and optional elements in Masses with children.

For student Masses, you may have an Introduction or Call to Worship before Mass begins. This can be read by the principal, a teacher or a senior student. All are welcomed and then invited to pray and participate. Any special intentions are mentioned.

Symbols may be brought up at this time, if they are not already in place. These symbols highlight the theme of the Mass or the liturgical season, such as a cornucopia or signs of harvest to represent Thanksgiving; an Advent wreath for Advent; sand and rocks for Lent; or flowers for the Easter season. Students of any age can carry these symbols. A reader can name the object and its significance as it is brought forward and placed before the altar, but this is entirely optional. The environment can also be prepared before the liturgy begins.

End this Introduction by announcing the opening hymn.

Introductory Rites

Mass begins with the Introductory Rites, which consist of the Entrance Procession and the Opening Hymn, the Penitential Act and the Opening Prayer. Since the Glory to God (Gloria) is reserved for Sundays, it is not usually part of school Masses.

The Entrance Procession

The priest and the altar servers process to the altar during the opening hymn. The assembly stands for the procession and sings.

The Penitential Act

In the Penitential Act, we ask God for forgiveness. It can take one of several forms: the Confiteor ("*I confess to almighty God and to you, my brothers and sisters…*"); "*Lord, have mercy…*"; or another prayer prescribed by the

Church. In a school weekday Mass, the priest may choose to omit this.

Opening Prayer

The Opening Prayer is the final part of the Introductory Rites. Here the priest calls upon the Father, the Son and the Holy Spirit. Although the words of the Opening Prayer change from one Mass to the next, it always begins with *"Let us pray"* and ends with the assembly saying, *"Amen."*

Liturgy of the Word

During the Liturgy of the Word, we are invited to listen to God's Word in the Bible. On Sundays, readings are taken from both the Old and New Testaments, and include the First Reading, the Responsorial Psalm, the Second Reading, and the Gospel. For weekday Masses (and therefore most school Masses), there is no second reading. The proclamation of the Word is followed by the homily. The Profession of Faith (the Creed) is usually omitted at weekday Masses. The Liturgy of the Word ends with the Prayer of the Faithful.

First Reading

All readings should be read from the Lectionary (the book of readings used at Mass). Select a reader to clearly proclaim the First Reading. The reader starts by saying, "A reading from …" At the end of the reading, the reader says, *"The word of the Lord."* All reply, *"Thanks be to God."* (See *Chapter 10* if you are choosing Mass readings.)

Responsorial Psalm

The Responsorial Psalm, which features verses and refrains, can be read but it is meant to be sung. Select an older student reader or cantor to lead this prayer. Ensure that they clearly indicate to the people when it is their turn to respond with the refrain. For school Masses, the refrain can be shown on an overhead or PowerPoint slide to help the students participate. There are seasonal psalms for Advent and Lent. Even if the verses are read, the refrain should be sung at school Masses.

Second Reading

As school Masses are usually during the week, there is no second reading. (See the *Directory for Masses with Children*, #42.)

Gospel Acclamation

The assembly is invited to stand for the Gospel Acclamation and the proclamation of the Gospel. The acclamation may be led by the choir or cantor. If you use a cantor, select a singer with a strong voice to properly herald the Gospel. During Lent, the word "Alleluia" is not used at Mass. Alternatives for Lent include *"Praise to you, Lord, king of eternal glory"* or *"Praise and honour to you, Lord Jesus Christ!"* Singing the Gospel Acclamation allows everyone to participate. If it is not sung, it is omitted.

Gospel

The presider begins by saying, *"The Lord be with you."* All respond, **"And with your spirit."** He continues, *"A reading from the holy Gospel according to... [Matthew, Mark, Luke, or John]."* All respond, **"Glory to you, O Lord."** We trace a cross on our forehead, lips and heart as we say these words, to signify that we remember God's word, we share it with others, and we keep it in our hearts. (Review this gesture with students sometime before the Mass.) After reading the Gospel, the priest says, *"The Gospel of the Lord."* All respond, **"Praise to you, Lord Jesus Christ."** The assembly then sits for the homily.

Homily

The homily, which relates the Scripture readings to our lives today, is given by the presider, usually from the ambo (the lectern from where the Scriptures are proclaimed). At school Masses, some priests like to move to the aisle or to the front of the altar to better connect with the students. Sometimes the priest chooses to engage the students through questions and responses as part of the homily.

With the priest's permission, someone who is not ordained may give the homily to children (see *Directory for Masses with Children*, #24).

Profession of Faith (the Creed)

As a rule, the Creed is not prescribed for weekday Masses, so you will not include it in school celebrations.

Prayer of the Faithful

The Prayer of the Faithful is a series of prayers the assembly offers for the Church, the world, those in need, and the community. See *Chapter 5* for some sample prayers.

To involve more students, you may want to choose a reader for each prayer if the priest agrees with this approach. If so, make sure they know exactly when to approach the microphone and are lined up in order, follow the same format when reading, and clearly indicate when the assembly is to respond, so these prayers are seamless. (If readers are of varying heights, consider using a handheld microphone that can be easily passed between readers, or a stepstool to give shorter students additional height. This prevents long pauses and noise resulting from microphone readjustments and ensures that each reader is heard.) The response to these prayers (such as "Lord, hear our prayer") may be sung or said.

Liturgy of the Eucharist

During the Liturgy of the Eucharist, using the words of the Eucharistic Prayer, the priest calls upon the Holy Spirit to change the bread and wine into the Body and Blood of Christ. The altar represents both a place of sacrifice and the table where we are fed. The Liturgy of the Eucharist begins with the Presentation of the Gifts (the Offertory), with an optional song, before moving into the Eucharistic Prayer, and ends with the Communion Rite.

Presentation of the Gifts

Students bring up the gifts of bread and wine to the altar. (As there is no collection of money at school Masses, no other offerings are brought to the altar. The exception is if students have taken part in a food drive; some of these gifts, which are truly offerings, may be carried up in the Offertory procession.) Often younger students fill this role. The presider takes the gifts and passes them to the altar servers. The gifts of bread and wine are placed on the altar, where the priest offers a prayer over them. He washes his hands with water to symbolize his desire to be cleansed from sin before preparing the Eucharist. During the Presentation of the Gifts, an Offertory song is often sung.

The Eucharistic Prayer

The priest then begins the Eucharistic Prayer of thanks and praise. This is the focus of the Mass, because here the bread and wine are changed into the Body and Blood of Christ. This prayer is led by the priest, but the people are actively involved in the prayers and responses within it.

Ask the priest to use one of the Eucharistic Prayers for Children, if possible. These texts are simpler and much easier for students to understand.

The three acclamations of the Eucharistic Prayer are meant to be sung. They may be led by the choir or a cantor.

• *Holy, Holy, Holy*

Holy, Holy, Holy Lord God of hosts.
Heaven and earth are full of your glory.
Hosanna in the highest.
Blessed is he who comes in the name of the Lord.
Hosanna in the highest.

• *Memorial Acclamation*

Priest: The mystery of faith.

All: We proclaim your Death, O Lord, and profess your Resurrection until you come again.

Or:

All: When we eat this Bread and drink this Cup, we proclaim your Death, O Lord, until you come again.

Or:

All: Save us, Saviour of the world, for by your Cross and Resurrection you have set us free.

• *Great Amen*

The Great Amen signals the end of the Eucharistic Prayer and is to be sung by the people immediately after the presider sings or says the doxology: "*Through him, and with him and in him, O God, almighty Father, in the unity of the Holy Spirit, all glory and honour is yours, forever and ever.*" The people respond, "*Amen.*"

The Communion Rite

• *Our Father*

This traditional prayer can be sung or said. The people stand to pray the Our Father.

• *Sign of Peace*

We are called to offer each other a sign of peace to show we are ready to eat at Christ's table. This action can take many forms. It may involve a simple nod of the head and a smile, a slight bow, or shaking hands and saying, "Peace be with you" or "The peace of Christ." It may be wise to invite students to exchange the peace only with two or three people near them.

• *Lamb of God*

The Lamb of God is to be sung by the assembly as the consecrated hosts are being prepared for distribution.

Lamb of God, you take away the sins of the world, have mercy on us.
Lamb of God, you take away the sins of the world, have mercy on us.
Lamb of God, you take away the sins of the world, grant us peace.

• *Holy Communion*

We are invited to eat at the Lord's table and receive the Body and Blood of Jesus. At school Masses, only the priest and sometimes the ministers of communion (teachers who distribute communion) will receive both the Body and Blood. Students usually receive only the consecrated bread.

Concluding Rites

The Concluding Rites are made up of the Blessing, Dismissal and procession out of the worship space.

Blessing

Sometimes the presider will wait in silence for a few moments before inviting the assembly to stand for the Blessing. This pause gives the people a chance to pray quietly after receiving communion. The words of the Blessing vary, but signal the end of the celebration. The assembly says *"Amen"* at the end.

Dismissal

The assembly remains standing as the priest sends them forth into the world. The people respond, *"Thanks be to God."*

Procession

During the closing hymn, the presider exits in procession with the altar servers. The members of the assembly wait until he has left the church and the closing hymn comes to an end before they exit.

*

If you are preparing a Mass, see *Appendix 1 – Mass Planning Guide* and *Mass Summary Sheet*. These easy-to-use organizational worksheets lead you step by step through the process. Once you have completed the itemized Mass Planning Guide, use the Summary Sheet as a quick reference tool for your celebration. These worksheets can be stored for future reference. (See *Chapter 12*.)

Notes

7

Teacher Participation

Why Is Teacher Participation Important?

Part of your vocation as a Catholic educator is to facilitate prayer in your school or classroom. Your guidance and support of students in their faith life are essential to your calling. Teacher participation is important for both prayer services and Masses. In preparing for community prayer, you take on the responsibilities of role model, leader, organizer, delegator and supervisor.

Good celebrations always require preparation and rehearsal. The first time you are asked to prepare a celebration, you might consult with someone who has done so before. As you begin, decide to be gentle with yourself. Do not attempt to prepare and carry out a large celebration on your first attempt. Start small. Start simply. Begin with minimal student involvement in small details and then gradually work your way up to more elaborate celebrations. Don't get discouraged if things don't work out the way you planned the first time. Learn from any miscues and turn any negativity into a learning opportunity.

Above all, remember that you are doing this to further the faith development of your students and to make it a meaningful experience for them.

Being a Role Model

In modelling proper behaviour, you will spend a great deal of time repeating instructions to your students on how to enter and exit a church for Mass or a prayer space for a prayer service, how to read clearly so all can understand, how to show the assembly when to respond, how to listen attentively, how to carry up the gifts of bread and wine in the Offertory, how to use a kneeler, how to pray the responses, and so much more. Be consistent in your directions and don't be disheartened if you feel like a broken record! The repeated messages will become a mantra for the students to follow, and eventually they will correct each other. This consistency will also carry over to future celebrations.

As a teacher, you also need to model good liturgy. Make sure celebrations are age appropriate. (See *Appendix 3 – Prayers and Prayer Services, Masses with Students.*) For older students, model how to write the Prayer of the Faithful so they can take on this job in the future.

Leadership

Your role will include leading the students in all practices – musical, reading, drama, dance or ritual, such as taking up the gifts at the Offertory or sharing the sign of peace. The first time you go through this process, no matter how old your students are, this will take a great deal of time.

Primary students need to be guided even more closely, both during the rehearsals and during the celebration. For many, it will be their first time in front of a large group, which can be intimidating. Knowing that you are nearby will do much to ease their nerves.

Set your students up for success. Take the time to patiently train each student in whatever role you have selected for them. Hold more than one run-through for each group of students. Have at least one rehearsal for each group in the space where you will be celebrating, using the same equipment and seating arrangements.

Organization

Preparing a celebration involves planning and arranging endless details, such as song selection; reading selection; singers; readers; equipment set-up; overheads or PowerPoint slides; song lyrics and prayers; and seating arrangements. Use an itemized list to ensure nothing has been forgotten. (See *Appendix 1 – Details List*.)

Delegating Tasks

Assign older students to carry out specific tasks as part of the planning and organization. Select students according to their strengths and inclinations. Try to include more students for each celebration. They will be happy to take on positions of responsibility.

Supervising

At the beginning, supervising all the student assignments will take a fair amount of time and energy. Each detail, each assignment, each job needs close supervision, especially when students are new to the task.

*

Planning a school liturgy can seem overwhelming at first, but if you train your students properly from the beginning, it will pay off. The practice and experience you and your students gain will serve as a great foundation for even more positive, spiritual and smooth-running celebrations in the future. It is always better to have fewer well-planned celebrations than numerous slipshod liturgies!

8

Student Participation

Why Is Student Participation Important?

As a Catholic educator, you are fortunate to be able to pray with your students, which allows you to engage them in expressing their faith in time-honoured traditions of the Church. You are shaping, guiding and watching your students as they grow in faith. They in turn can express their faith in their own way and actively grow in a familiar environment with their peers.

School liturgies give students an opportunity to get involved in various liturgical ministries and learn the Mass prayers and responses, even if their families are not involved in their parish community.

Encourage student participation by making it an inviting experience. You'll find that students who get involved have a greater sense of belonging, are more engaged in expressing their faith at their own comfort level, and take ownership of and pride in their accomplishments. Many will take these positive faith-filled experiences to heart and start to get involved at their own parish. They will also learn more about the tenets and traditions of their faith. As they grow older, they can take on leadership roles in communal liturgies and be encouraged to pass this knowledge on to others.

Engaging Students in Liturgies

To get students interested in participating in school liturgies, highlight things that are relevant to them. While younger students may like prayer services about Halloween or Spring, older students have other priorities, including peer relationships, school clubs and social justice. Knowing your students' interests and aligning your prayer services with these pursuits will go a long way to engaging and piquing their interest. There are many resources available with ready-made prayer services that address these issues. (See *Appendix 3 – Prayer Services*.)

Celebrating the liturgical year, such as the seasons of Advent, Christmas, Lent and Easter, is appropriate for everyone. You will likely celebrate in these seasons with a school Mass. Make sure you take into account the age, maturity and interests of your students when planning and preparing.

Every student has a role to play as a member of the assembly. They need to know when to respond and what to say, when to kneel and when to stand, when to sing and what words to use, when to listen and when to pray.

Encourage them to take on other roles when they are ready. They will come to appreciate prayer services and Masses not merely as random words, but as *their* celebrations of prayer, developed from their toil, their imagination, their energy, their faith. They will see themselves reflected in the face of God.

Student Roles

Students can get involved in a range of roles:

- write the Prayer of the Faithful
- write short prayers for prayer services
- select songs
- sing in a choir or as a cantor
- play an instrument
- be a greeter or usher
- proclaim God's Word
- be an altar server
- set up and take down microphones, music stands and the overhead projector and screen
- put up the overheads or run PowerPoint slides
- look after the CDs or mp3 player
- bring up symbolic items before the celebration begins to set the environment or to put student art on the walls
- bring up the gifts of bread and wine at the Offertory
- mentor younger students
- do a liturgical dance or drama (for prayer services)

General Guidelines

All students who have specific roles in the Mass or prayer service should have a copy of the order of service to follow so they know exactly when they are needed. Students feel most comfortable when they know what to expect and are confident that there will be few surprises. Be consistent in giving directions

for specific tasks; this will serve as long-term training and carry over from one celebration to the next. Depending on the age of the students, a full dress rehearsal may be warranted.

Writing

In coaching your students to write short prayers or the Prayer of the Faithful, give them clear and simple guidelines to follow. (See *Chapter 5, Chapter 6* and *Appendix 1*.) For students to be successful, they need sample prayers to follow. Make sure the task does not seem too onerous. Brainstorm ideas with them to get them started. Monitor and track their progress, offering your support as needed, but avoid changing their wording to reflect your personal word choices. As long as they have followed the guidelines and their message is clear, let them express themselves in their own way, or have classes write the Prayer of the Faithful as a communal effort.

Proclaiming God's Word or Reading the Prayers

Select your readers carefully. It will not enhance the celebration for the assembly or boost a student's confidence if you give them a long or difficult reading. Select readers who can proclaim the Word of God and the prayers clearly, for all to hear. Lots of practice is essential, especially if they will be using a microphone. Coach students to read aloud slowly, carefully and with expression.

Slowly: Whatever the students are reading, it should feel almost too slow in practice. Nerves on the actual day of the service will speed up their reading, so get them to read as slowly as possible during practice sessions. This ensures that every word is said and that no syllables are swallowed. Speaking quickly when using a microphone will make it hard for those listening to understand.

Carefully: Make sure your students can pronounce every word they are to read; know which syllables to stress and where to pause. Above all, confirm that they fully understand everything they are reading. If the reader does not understand what they are saying, the assembly will not understand what they are hearing. Also, ensure that they are proclaiming Scripture from a lectionary (not a missalette), even if this means you type the reading using a large font and paperclip it into a lectionary. If the student is reading a prayer out loud, put the page in a booklet or on heavy card stock to give them dignity, rather than scribbling them on paper, which can rattle.

With expression: Encourage them to add expression. The more expression they inject into their reading, the more engaged the listeners will be when they hear it. If a response is required from the assembly, be sure the reader knows how to indicate this clearly. A raised arm or hand is usually enough. Remind them that reading aloud in a classroom is very different from reading in a gym or a church. The acoustics and the size of the assembly will markedly alter the projection, volume and presentation style. If possible, practise in the space where the celebration will be held, using any microphones or stands that will be required. Practising will help to calm the nerves of new readers and reinforce the confidence of more experienced ones.

Music

A class or school choir adds a lot to a liturgical celebration. Ensure that the music you select is appropriate in content and easy to sing.

Primary choirs generally do not feature soloists; instead, they promote singing by the whole assembly using songs with simple, repeated refrains. Projecting the words on an overhead allows everyone to join in. To teach younger children song lyrics, use simple actions for the refrains and repeated patterns to help them participate actively.

In junior choirs, some students may sing a verse alone or play an instrument at the celebration. Give them a complete copy of the service as well as their music so they know exactly where they fit in. Decide ahead of time when they will receive communion (before or after they begin their songs), what they will do with their instruments at that time, and what path they will take to return to their positions or their seats after communion.

While live music is preferred for Masses, it is not always possible. When no musician is available, play the music on a CD or mp3 player to accompany your students. Make sure the recorded music does not overpower the assembly.

Rehearsal time is essential for all singers and musicians. Have at least one rehearsal in the space where the Mass or prayer service will be held. Have on hand everything you will use on the day of the celebration, including instruments, CD player or mp3 player, CD, music stands, microphones, overheads and projector or laptop and PowerPoint slides, and seating arranged for the choir, musicians or cantors. This will do much to alleviate students' nerves.

It is also important to have a song practice with the entire student body before the liturgy. In some schools, this is done by class or division. The assembly can't be expected to sing and participate if they don't know the songs. Singing by a choir alone is not usually appropriate at school Masses.

Within the liturgy, repetition of a refrain helps everyone participate. Use acclamations from one Mass setting, where the tune is similar, rather than choosing acclamations from several settings. Choose a communion song that students can sing in procession without a hymnbook. Use many of the same pieces of music in future celebrations rather than trying to introduce new ones each time.

For information on choosing music, see *Chapter 10*. For a list of hymns, see *Appendix 2*.

Drama and Dance

Most Masses do not incorporate dance or drama, but these can be used in prayer services to enhance the prayerful attitude of the participants to great effect.

Tableaux or silent movement are very effective and can be a valuable storytelling tool for any age. Younger students enjoy acting out readings, which works well for many Bible stories (e.g., the Prodigal Son, the Christmas story). Keep the costumes simple, avoiding headdresses that obstruct students' vision or long robes that could cause them to trip. Use props that will not break, scatter or roll when dropped.

Liturgical dance can add grace and solemnity to prayer, and students enjoy watching it.

Many resources are available for liturgical dance and drama. (See *Appendix 3 – Liturgical Dance*.) If you choose these options, ensure that the costuming, choreography and actions are conducive to the prayerful atmosphere you wish to create. Students should know when to have costumes or music ready as well as where they need to be before and after they perform. Drama or dance should always complement the celebration, rather than being the central focus.

Symbols

At some Masses and prayer services, symbols that reflect the liturgical season are placed in the liturgical space or may be carried up just before things get under way. A reader may describe the symbol and how it relates to the celebration. (See notes on Symbols for Prayer

Services in *Chapter 5* and for Masses in *Chapter 6*). Make sure that those bringing up the symbols know where to place them and where to go afterwards. After the celebration, have someone collect the symbols and return them to their proper place. If you wish, place them in a prominent place in the school to remind your students of the time you spent together in prayer.

The Offertory

Students may carry the bread and wine in the Offertory procession and hand them to the priest. These will become the Body and Blood of Jesus. Note that the water that will be used within the Eucharistic Prayer is not carried in procession. If the school community has collected money for a specific cause or items for a food drive (such as for an Advent or Lenten project), this could be part of the procession. Make sure the presider knows about it beforehand.

Serving at the Altar

Being an altar server at Mass is a rewarding experience for many students. Their primary role is to assist the priest at the altar. Servers are students who have celebrated First Communion; priests often prefer that they have already been trained to serve in their home parish. Some priests will offer on-the-job training, while others like to instruct the altar servers before the Mass.

Servers carry the processional cross and candles, hold the Missal (the book of Mass prayers) for the priest, may ring bells at certain points in the Eucharistic Prayer (optional), and bring water, a linen cloth and other items to the priest during the preparation of the gifts.

During Mass, the servers sit near the priest and actively participate in the liturgy by singing the hymns, saying the responses, and sitting, kneeling or standing at the appropriate times. After Mass, they extinguish any candles that were lit for the celebration and help with the general clean-up.

Student Mentoring

Liturgical celebrations are a great opportunity for older students to mentor younger ones. These older students can sit with the younger ones during the celebration, help them with reading, dance or drama at practices, or guide them when it is time to participate. The older ones are able to model good behaviour and show when to sit, stand, pray, kneel, sing and respond to the prayers. Younger students look up to them as role models, which often prompts both groups to show more mature behaviour. This mixed seating arrangement can help teaching staff with supervision duties as well.

Notes

9

Postures, Rituals and Responses

This chapter deals with the appropriate postures, rituals and responses for student community prayer and best practices for preparing students to take part in prayer services and Masses.

Arrival, Entry and Seating

1. Before the Mass or prayer service begins, make sure that all students have gone to the bathroom, had their drinks or snacks, and tidied their desks so they can focus on the celebration.

2. If the celebration is being held in the church and the weather is wet or snowy, leave plenty of time to get your students dressed and to the church. For younger classes, enlist the help of older students.

3. Remind students to enter the church or prayer space in a quiet, respectful and orderly fashion. If you are using the gym, all-purpose room, library or a classroom, this may confuse younger students who expect to do the things they usually do in that space. Entering the space calmly will help to set the mood for prayer.

4. If you will celebrate in the church, invite students to bless themselves silently by dipping their fingers in the holy water at the entrance and then making the sign of the cross before finding a seat in the pews. Model this for younger students.

5. In school locations, students might sit on chairs, on the floor or on mats. A day or two before the celebration, have them practise entering the space and sitting down quietly.

6. Staff members should decide on seating ahead of time for all grades to avoid confusion. Include enough seating for planned special guests or family members who may be attending. Assigned seating provides consistency and makes it possible for everyone to have a view.

7. Seat your readers in sequence so they may go up to the ambo (lectern) easily. Students who will bring up gifts, act as cantors or take part in a liturgical drama or dance should be seated at the end of a row for easy exit and entry.

8. If any students or guests require special seating for any reason, arrange this ahead of time.

9. Seat the choir where they will have a clear view of lyrics and the choir director and will be able to lead the assembly in singing.

10. Consider recruiting student volunteers from the older grades to sit with younger peers. Ask colleagues teaching

these grades to recommend responsible students. The younger students enjoy having role models, and the older students enjoy the responsibility of mentoring younger ones.

11. Once students are seated, encourage them to sit quietly and wait patiently for everyone else to enter and sit down. Primary students often sit at the front, but you may want to save their space and have them seated last as they can find it hard to sit still while waiting.

Postures During Mass

We stand, sit and kneel at various times during the Mass. Each posture is done for a specific reason. As practices do vary somewhat from one diocese to another, check with the local parish to find out what the practice is in your diocese.

Standing

1. We stand for the gathering and final processions.

2. During Mass, we stand for the reading of the Gospel, because we are listening to the words and stories of Christ himself.

3. We usually stand when we pray the Creed, some of the Eucharistic Prayer, the Lord's Prayer and other prayers. Sometimes at school Masses not held in a church, the students remain seated for the Eucharistic Prayer.

Sitting

1. We sit when we listen to the first and second readings.

2. During Mass, we sit when we listen to the homily. We are called to hear with

open hearts and pay attention to what the priest is saying to us.

3. During a prayer service, we sit and listen attentively to a reflection or an explanation of the reading or theme of the service.

Kneeling

1. When we kneel, we show reverence and humility.

2. During Mass, we kneel during parts of the Eucharistic Prayer, when the Holy Spirit changes our gifts of bread and wine into the Body and Blood of Christ.

3. Many people kneel in prayer before Mass begins. Students are welcome to offer their own silent prayers of thanksgiving, supplication or hope, or to ask for forgiveness, as they kneel.

4. To maintain the prayerful and respectful mood, kneelers should be raised and lowered quietly.

Genuflecting and Bowing

The following postures are used only in a church.

1. We genuflect by briefly bending one leg until the knee touches the floor. We genuflect to the tabernacle, which contains the Blessed Sacrament (the Body of Christ). This action is usually accompanied by the sign of the cross.

2. Before entering the pew to sit down, we bow to the altar. We do the same as we leave the pew at the end of Mass.

3. In some churches, when readers approach the ambo to proclaim the Word of God, they pause briefly at the steps to the altar and bow to the altar as a sign of reverence. Find out if this is the

practice in the parish church where you will celebrate.

4. Students who bring up symbols to the altar before Mass or to the prayer focal point during a prayer service should process up the main aisle to the front and hand the item to another student, teacher or principal, or simply place the symbol there. At church, they should bow to the altar before they return to their seats, if this is the practice for that parish.

5. Students who bring the gifts of bread and wine to the altar at Mass should process up the main aisle to the front of the church and give these to the priest (who will hand them to the altar servers). Then the gift bearers should bow to the priest before returning to their seats.

6. Younger students are often given the responsibility of bringing up symbols or gifts, since they are not ready to lead prayers, proclaim readings or sing in the choir. Be sure to practise processing and bowing with these students.

The Assembly's Responses

1. Prepare your students to participate fully in reciting or singing the responses for the Mass or prayer service. For prayer services, simple, repetitive responses work best, especially for younger students. Consider using overheads or PowerPoint slides to help the community participate.

2. For Masses, most of the prayers and responses are prescribed. There is not always time or opportunity to assemble the entire school for a practice run.

Instead, distribute copies of the Mass responses to all staff members to practise with their own students. On the day of the Mass, consider using overheads or PowerPoint slides containing the responses for students to follow.

3. Some responses are sung instead of spoken. Practise with your choir or class (and with the entire student community, if you can) beforehand to ensure wide participation.

4. Most Mass responses do not change from one celebration to the next, but the Responsorial Psalm changes every day. Make sure the Psalm refrain is easy to remember, or that everyone can see the words to follow along.

5. In order for sung responses to add to your celebration, make sure everyone knows the tune and the words. Take the time to teach the music properly. Have a choir or cantor lead the assembly in song.

6. If students are leading the Responsorial Psalm or the Prayer of the Faithful, make sure they clearly indicate when the assembly is to respond. Raising one arm is one way to cue the assembly.

Exchanging the Sign of Peace

1. When we offer the sign of peace during Mass, we are telling those near us that we want them to live in Christ's peace, knowing that the Lord is with them always. This is a serious and sincere moment.

2. Limit this exchange to the person on either side of each student to avoid having them stretching across the pews to

reach all their friends. Voices should not be raised.

3. Students shake hands and say to each other, "Peace be with you" or "The peace of Christ." (In cold and flu season especially, students can bow or nod rather than shaking hands.)

4. The sign of peace should be carried out quietly and quickly so it does not disrupt the flow of the Mass.

5. Have primary students practise this ritual ahead of time so they know what to expect when it happens during Mass.

Receiving Communion

1. Most students attending Catholic schools have celebrated their First Communion by the end of Grade 2, and so will be familiar with processing up the aisle for communion. Those who are receiving communion should fold their hands together as in prayer and not touch other students. In some places, children who are not baptized or who have not yet celebrated First Communion approach the priest in the Communion procession for a blessing. This is a fairly recent practice. If children receive good formation and instruction about why they don't approach the table of the Eucharist, they do not need to be part of the procession. (After all, everyone receives a blessing at the end of Mass!) Talk to the priest about it beforehand so you are both on the same page.

2. When those receiving reach the front of the line, they place one hand under the other, with palms up. The priest or minister of communion says, "The Body of Christ." The student responds, "Amen." The priest or minister of communion places the host in the student's palm, then the student immediately places the host in their mouth before returning to their seat. They are not to take the host out of their mouth for any reason, and must consume it entirely.

3. When going up to receive communion, students need to patiently wait their turn before leaving their pew, remembering to allow for the pew in front to empty first before they join the procession.

4. Make sure students know which way to go up to communion and return to their seats: up the centre aisle and down a side aisle, or up the outside of the centre aisle and down the inside of the centre aisle. Use whichever practice best suits your needs and the space. Sometimes in Masses in the gym, the minister of communion may go to the students rather than the students processing. This will depend on the seating arrangements and the number of students present.

The most appropriate response to the Eucharist is to stand and join in the communion hymn as a sign of our unity until everyone has received communion. Then there is a brief time of silent reflection before the Prayer after Communion.

Leaving the Worship Space

1. After the priest or other leader has processed out, we prepare to exit. We have heard the Word of God, we have prayed and, in the case of Mass, we have received Jesus in the Eucharist. As we

process out, we continue to sing the closing hymn. We are sent forth to love and serve!

2. At church, students should exit their pews and briefly face the front of the church. If the tabernacle is visible in the main worship space, they genuflect. If it is not visible in the main worship space, they bow to the altar. Then they make the sign of the cross before leaving, quietly turn towards the doors of the church and follow their teachers to the exit.

3. At school, especially if students are seated on the floor, have them stand as a class first, then line up and proceed quickly and quietly to the exit behind their teacher.

Reviewing the Experience

1. After all Masses and prayer services, review the experience with your students at an age-appropriate level.

2. Review what students recall from the celebration. This can be done in a question-and-answer format or as an open discussion:

• What do you remember most?

• What helped you to pray/participate?

• What made it difficult or hindered you from participating?

• What should we repeat next time? What should we change?

• What will you do now to share the Good News?

3. Keep track of their ideas for next time.

The more prepared your students are for what they will experience, the more they will get out of it. Practise, model and prepare well to enrich each celebration.

Notes

10

How to Prepare or Find Readings and Music

This chapter will help you choose readings and music for a school Mass or prayer service. Many resources contain ready-to-use prayer services on various themes that are age appropriate – see *Appendix 3 – Prayer Services and Masses* – but if you would like to tailor one of these to your situation or write your own prayer service from scratch, you need to know where to look.

Selecting Readings and Responsorial Psalms

To frame your initial search, start by consulting the Ordo. This is the liturgical calendar of the Church. For each day of the year, the Ordo lists the liturgical season and colour, feasts, saints' days, and any special rites or devotions to be celebrated on that day. Many schools and all parishes have copies of this helpful reference.

Scripture readings

The Scripture readings for each day are listed in the Ordo and found in the Lectionary. This is the large book of readings used at Mass, and is available in a smaller version for individuals to buy. The readings may also be found in the *Living with Christ* missalette. You can also look up the readings in a Children's Lectionary. All parishes and many schools have copies.

Remember that the prescribed daily weekday readings can be changed for Masses with children. (See the *Directory for Masses with Children*, #42.)

Since prayer services do not follow a prescribed format, there is more leeway in selecting readings for the service. For Masses, most priests will allow schools to use readings that fit the liturgical season (such as Advent or Easter) rather than limiting them to the Mass of the day, if the readings are not appropriate for younger children. Also, if the date of the Mass changes at the last minute, you will not have to prepare new readings. Consult a daily or Sunday missal to find readings that fit the season.

Selecting readings based on a particular theme also allows the school community to highlight faith and secular events that shape the school year. (See the list in *Chapter 1*.)

To choose readings, check a Bible concordance, which indexes topics and readings alphabetically, or other publications that organize readings by theme. (See *Appendix 3 – Resources – Where to Find Things in the Bible*.) Some bibles contain a subject index at the back. Online resources are also helpful. Whatever readings you choose, make sure to check with the priest well before your celebration about the choices. This will give you ample time to practise and prepare with your students. If the priest suggests alternate readings, you will have time to meet with him and choose different ones. The priest prepares his homily based on the readings, so he needs to know well in advance of the liturgy which ones will be proclaimed.

The Bible is available in many English translations. It is best to use the New Revised Standard Version (NRSV), the translation used in Canadian parishes, for liturgies. (The Good News version is appropriate for religious education and formal catechesis with children.) Make sure the readings you choose contain appropriate language and content for your students.

Responsorial Psalms

The Lectionary, daily missalette and Sunday missal contain the Responsorial Psalms that go with the readings of the day. If you choose a different reading, you may wish to use a different Responsorial Psalm as well. Many hymnals (see *Appendix 2*) organize Responsorial Psalms by season and liturgical year. Each psalm is paired with an appropriate Gospel

Acclamation, which is helpful. Responsorial Psalms may be read or sung, but if the Gospel Acclamation is not sung, it is omitted. There are seasonal psalms for Advent and Lent.

Prayers and responses

Mass prayers and responses are found in the Roman Missal and in daily missalettes and the small Sunday missal.

Selecting Music

Why include music?

St. Augustine said that "To sing is to pray twice," meaning that if you sing with all your heart and direct it to God, you pray not only with your words but with your voice as well. Good music that is liturgically appropriate and aesthetically pleasing adds so much to a liturgy and involves the whole assembly. You do not need accomplished musicians, but the music should be on key, heartfelt, prayerful and directed to God, and accessible to the assembly.

The music during any faith celebration should not distract from worship, but instead is integral to the liturgy, liturgical season and appointed Scriptures, and fosters participation of the faithful. For example, the opening hymn is about gathering as one, assembling the people of God and bringing in a sense of unity. The communion hymn "is to express the communicants' union in spirit by means of the unity of their voices, to show joy of heart, and to highlight more clearly the 'communitarian' nature of the procession to receive Communion." (General Instruction of the Roman Missal, #86) Keep in mind the purpose of each hymn to help you select appropriate ones.

Liturgical versus secular music

While the primary aim of secular melodies is to entertain, music in a religious celebration should help the assembly to pray and to praise God and should reflect the Scripture readings, liturgical season, prayers and the liturgical action. The music you choose can be solemn, traditional, contemporary or joyful, depending on the liturgical season and the readings, as long as the words and the music are prayerfully directed to God.

Two categories of music for Mass

Two categories of music at Mass are the parts of the Mass and the hymns or songs. The responses to the Mass prayers are the first priority.

Many musical settings are available for the parts of the Mass: these include the Kyrie (Lord, Have Mercy), the Glory to God, the Responsorial Psalm, the Gospel Acclamation, the Prayer of the Faithful, the Holy, Holy, Holy, the Memorial Acclamation, the Great Amen, the Our Father and the Lamb of God. (See *Appendix 2*.) This music is often responsorial, alternating between the choir, the cantor or the priest and the assembly, although some are complete pieces unto themselves.

Most are sung only at Mass. While most of them can be recited rather than sung, the Gospel Acclamation is omitted entirely if it is not sung.

Hymns are sung during the Entrance Procession, the Offertory, Communion and the Recessional Procession. These times of the Mass involve movement. For Communion, select a hymn with a refrain that students can sing without a hymnbook. The music chosen should reflect what is happening in the liturgy: processing to receive the Body and Blood of Christ (for example, "Taste and See" or "Take and Eat"). Aim for as much singing by the assembly as possible.

Although almost any musical instrument can be used in liturgical celebrations, it must not take away from the focus of the celebration. When accompanying vocalists, the instruments must not overpower the voices.

General guidelines for selecting music

When preparing music for a community liturgy, certain guidelines will help you make decisions. Take into account the availability and abilities of musicians, the music that is available and how the words will be shown, and the music the community knows, so that as many people as possible will sing. Above all, make sure the lyrics and the way the music is played and sung are respectful, faith-filled and prayerful. Secular music, however inspiring it may be, is not appropriate for Mass. A wide range of hymn styles – from traditional to contemporary – is available, so choose what works for your setting. For prayer services, you have more flexibility, but make sure that the words are appropriate for a faith context. You are seeking songs of thankfulness, praise, supplication and devotion to God, which are communal expressions rather than personal ones.

Remember that music in the liturgy is never a performance or form of entertainment, and should not be the focus of any liturgy. Instead, music complements the liturgical action, draws the faithful into prayer and praise, and is integral to the liturgy.

Music choices

A list of some of the most familiar hymns is found in *Appendix 2*.

As children have higher voices than most adults, you may need to change the key (raise it) so students can sing along.

Whatever music you select, make sure your students will understand what they are singing, will believe in the songs' messages, and will express their faith with enthusiasm in song. Having a prayerful attitude and a heart that is open to receiving the Word of God are the keys to a good experience of liturgy. If music heightens this experience, then it has fulfilled its purpose.

A well-balanced prayer service or Mass is made up of good music, sound liturgy and clear pastoral messages. After celebrating together, people should leave feeling satisfied, with their hearts full of song and their spirits nourished by the Word of God.

11

What Else? Details, Details!

Once you have chosen the location, selected the readings and music, and prepared your students for the Mass or prayer service, working out some final details will help your celebration to run smoothly and be meaningful.

Is Everything There?

1. Whether you are preparing for a Mass at the church or a prayer service in the school gym, arrange ahead of time to transport what you will need on the day.

2. Give a copy of your Details Checklist (see *Appendix 1*) to the person who is transporting the items for your celebration. Before it leaves the school, ensure that all electronic equipment you will be using is working.

Set-up

1. When setting up a screen for overheads or PowerPoint slides, make sure the screen does not obstruct the view of the altar or the prayer focal point.

2. Know the location of any electrical outlets for CD players, mp3 docks and speakers, overhead projector, laptop or other electrical equipment you may be using.

3. Bring the correct type and length of extension cord. Place it so that no one will trip over it.

4. Use a small table or chair for the overhead projector or laptop, if needed.

5. Place overheads or PowerPoint slides containing hymn lyrics or group responses in the correct order. Seat readers in order, too.

6. Test all equipment once you have plugged it in.

7. If you are using recorded music, make sure the CD player or mp3 player is easily accessible to the choir director or musicians. Bring a backup copy of the recorded music.

8. Check that the sound system is on. Check the levels.

9. Set up the microphones and music stands. Test the mikes.

Lighting

1. Know where the light switches are.

2. Lights need to be bright to enable safe entry and exit for students, staff and guests.

3. Overheads and PowerPoint slides, however, are most visible in dim light. Bring a small flashlight so you can safely operate equipment without disruption.

4. If you are using candles, have matches or a lighter on hand. (Barbecue lighters work well.) Designate someone responsible to light them before your celebration begins.

Packing Up

1. Use your Details Checklist as you pack up all the equipment so nothing is left behind.
2. Turn off the sound system and return the microphones to their proper place.
3. Return any other borrowed equipment.

Oops! What to Do When Things Go Wrong

No matter how well you plan, setbacks, illness, absences or technical difficulties may happen. Remain calm. You can be prepared for most contingencies.

1. Bring extra copies of all lyrics, readings, the Details Checklist and the complete order of service.
2. Prepare and bring a backup CD and a copy of the PowerPoint slides.
3. Select at least one backup reader, cantor, musician and symbol bearer. For Mass, also have a backup gift bearer, minister of communion and altar server.
4. Ensure that the choir can lead the music and the readers can lead the group responses in case the overhead projector or laptop do not work and you cannot project hymn lyrics or group responses.
5. If the microphones or sound system stop working, ask the assembly for their cooperation in being extra quiet so the readers can be heard.

12

How to Archive Materials

Archive the prayer services and Masses you have prepared so you or other staff members can refer to them in the future. Place the following items in three-ring binders (by theme, by liturgical season, or whatever system works for you) and keep them in a central spot, such as the principal's office or the library. Include an itemized table of contents for each binder. Catalogue the binders so they are easy to use.

1. Print a labelled paper copy of each prayer service and Mass. Include the Summary Sheets and Planning Guides.

2. File sheet music, song lyrics and their overheads by liturgical season and alphabetically by title so they are easy to find.

3. Store the various Mass prayers and responses on overheads according to their liturgical season. Number the overheads to keep them in the correct order.

4. Archive a copy of your PowerPoint presentation on a CD or DVD.

5. Store music CDs and CD or DVD copies of PowerPoint slides in ready-made folders, available at most office supply stores. These folders can be inserted into three-ring binders. Make sure the disks are clearly labelled. For music CDs, list all the titles in order directly on each CD.

6. All of the above items can also be backed up on labelled USB drives. Store your USB drives and paper copies separately.

Your prayer services and Masses will now be readily available and will offer several accessible options for school staff.

Liturgies that are well planned and well prepared help the community to pray and praise God together. Everyone understands what they should be doing and when, and is drawn into the celebration!

Notes

Appendix 1

Master Worksheets

Mass Planning Guide

Date of Mass: _____

Music Outline: *For the Mass you will need to select 4 songs:*

Gathering: _____

Instrument(s): _____

CD: _____ **Track number:** ____

- -

Offertory: _____

Instrument(s): _____

CD: _____ **Track number:** ____

- -

Communion: _____

Instrument(s): _____

CD: _____ **Track number:** ____

- -

Recessional: _____

Instrument(s): _____

CD: _____ **Track number:** ____

- -

(Make sure you communicate this information to the priest beforehand.)

These lists are also available for download at www.schools.novalis.ca/SchoolLiturgiesMadeEasy.html

For each part of the Mass below, indicate: **"choir,"** **"cantor (add name)"** or **"said".**

Lord, Have Mercy: _____

Responsorial Psalm: _____

Gospel Acclamation: _____
(Note: if it is not sung, the Gospel Acclamation is omitted.)

Choose one musical setting for the following acclamations:
Prayer of the Faithful: _____

Holy, Holy, Holy (sung): _____

Memorial Acclamation (sung): _____

Great Amen (sung): _____

Our Father: _____

Lamb of God (sung – is usually from the same musical setting as the acclamations):
_____

Call to Worship: Read by: _____

Decide who will read the introduction. The Call to Worship
- welcomes all who have gathered
- outlines the theme of the celebration
- if there are no symbols (see below) being brought up, ends by announcing the opening hymn.

Optional:

Offerings or Symbols

These highlight one aspect of the celebration. A few symbolic items are best displayed in front of the altar before Mass begins, as part of the environment when the space is prepared. If you decide to have these items carried in a procession before the celebration begins, you may want a reader to comment on each one. If these items are carried up during the Opening Hymn, it is best to do so without the comments, to avoid interfering with the liturgical action that has begun. (Note that only the gifts of bread and wine are to be brought up as part of the Offertory procession.)

Sample offering comments (optional):

1. We bring a bible to remind us of the Word of God and the faith we share as a community.

2. We bring this tambourine to remind us of the songs we sing together in praising God.

3. We bring these flowers to remind us of our friendships, which will blossom and be strengthened by God's love during this school year.

4. We bring a globe to remind us that no matter where we are, we must continue to reach out to others to share our love and faith.

Offerings or Symbols   Read by: _____

Brought up by: _____

_____

Offering # 1: _____

_____

_____

Offering #2: _____

_____

_____

Offering #3: _____

_____

_____

Offering #4: _____

_____

_____

Introductory Rites:

Invite those gathered to sing together:

Let us all now join in our opening hymn: [hymn title]

Liturgy of the Word

First Reading: **Proclaimed(read)by:**_____

Use the reading from the Mass of the day or, if the priest agrees, select an appropriate Scripture reading. (Include the book, chapter and verses: e.g., Isaiah 12:12-21, 24.) Note: Weekday Masses have only one reading before the Gospel.

_____

_____

Responsorial Psalm: **Sung/Read by:**_____

Use the Psalm for the day, or if the priest agrees, select an appropriate Psalm.
(Be sure to include the psalm number and the verses you will use: e.g., Psalm 19:1-4.)

Response: _____

_____

Verse 1:

_____

_____

_____

Verse 2:

_____

_____

Verse 3:

_____

_____

Verse 4:

_____

_____

Gospel Acclamation   **Sung by:**_____

(Note: If you select your Responsorial Psalm from the *Catholic Book of Worship III*, you will find that each one is paired with an appropriate Gospel Acclamation verse. Omit the Gospel Acclamation if you are not going to sing it.)

_____

_____

Gospel

The priest will proclaim the Gospel. Use the Gospel of the day or, if the priest agrees, select an appropriate Gospel reading. (Include the book, chapter and verses: e.g., John 2:13-25.)

_____

_____

Prayer of the Faithful: **Read by:**_____

_____

_____

_____

The response is: _____.

1. *Needs of the Church*

_____

_____

_____

2. *Public authorities, teachers, priests, principals*

_____

_____

_____

3. *For those oppressed by any need … the sick and those who care for them, the poor, the hungry, the lonely*

_____

_____

_____

    These lists are also available for download at www.schools.novalis.ca/SchoolLiturgiesMadeEasy.html

4. *For the local community; can include those gathered*

_____

_____

_____

5. *Optional: for those who have died*

_____

_____

_____

To see the completed Mass 'at a glance', fill in the **Mass Summary Sheet**.

Mass Summary Sheet

(to use on the day of the celebration)

Date of Mass: _____

Before Mass Begins		
Optional: Symbols are brought up		Brought up by:
Introduction		By:

Part of the Mass	Song/Reading	Proclaimed/Sung by
Introductory Rites		
Opening Hymn		All
Penitential Act (Lord, Have Mercy)		All
Opening Prayer		The priest
Liturgy of the Word		
First Reading		
Responsorial Psalm		
Gospel Acclamation (omitted if not sung)		
Gospel (from Matthew, Mark, Luke or John)		The priest
Homily		The priest
Prayer of the Faithful		

These lists are also available for download at www.schools.novalis.ca/SchoolLiturgiesMadeEasy.html

Liturgy of the Eucharist		
Offertory Hymn (optional)		All
Presentation of the Gifts		
Eucharistic Prayer		The priest
Holy, Holy, Holy		All
Memorial Acclamation		All
Great Amen		All
Our Father		All
Lamb of God		All
Communion Hymn(s)		All
Concluding Rites		
Closing Prayer/Dismissal		The priest
Recessional Hymn		All

Other Roles for Mass

Overhead projector:
(set-up)

1. _____

Microphones (set-up):

1. _____

2. _____

Overheads or
PowerPoint slides:

1. _____

2. _____

CD player or
mp3 player:

1. _____

Transportation of
equipment (if needed):

1. _____

2. _____

Extraordinary
Ministers
of Communion:

1. _____

2. _____

3. _____

Altar servers:

1. _____

2. _____

3. _____

These lists are also available for download at www.schools.novalis.ca/SchoolLiturgiesMadeEasy.html

Prayer Service Planning Guide

Title of Prayer Service: _____

Offerings or Symbols Accompanying text read by: _____

          Brought up by: _____

          _____

Offering #1: _____

_____

_____

Offering #2: _____

_____

_____

Offering #3: _____

_____

_____

Offering #4: _____

_____

_____

Introduction: Read by:_____

1. Decide who will read the introduction.
2. Begin with the sign of the cross.
3. Welcome all who have come to join in the prayer service.
4. You may wish to add any special intentions here.
5. Outline the theme of the prayer service.
6. End with the announcement of the Opening Song.

_____

_____

_____

Opening Song: _____

Cantor(s): _____

Instrument(s): _____

CD: _____   Track number: _____

Scripture Reading: **Proclaimed by:** _____

Select an appropriate reading for the theme you have chosen.
(Include the book, chapter and verses: e.g., 1 Corinthians 12:12-21, 26-27.)

_____

_____

Prayer of the Faithful: **Read by:** _____

_____

_____

_____

The response is: _____.

1. *Needs of the Church*

_____

_____

_____

2. *Public authorities, teachers, priests, principals*

_____

_____

_____

3. *For those oppressed by any need…the sick and those who care for them, the poor,
   the hungry, the lonely.*

_____

_____

_____

4. *For the local community; can include those gathered*

_____

_____

_____

_____

5. *Optional: for those who have died*

_____

_____

_____

Litany (optional):

The structures of litanies can vary. The purpose is to ensure that all are included in some sort of shared prayer. Litanies are often used when there is no homily. (They can be replaced by a prepared reflection.) To ensure that many are included, either go with a structure similar to the Prayer of the Faithful, where there is a repeated phrase and a leader of prayers, or divide the group into left and right groups or select many readers to read different parts. The Litany can be one of the most difficult but most rewarding prayers to write.

_____

_____

_____

_____

_____

_____

_____

Additional Song (optional): _____

Cantor(s): _____

Instrument(s): _____

CD: _____   Track number: ____

Liturgical Dance (optional):   **Dancers:** _____

                                          _____

                                          Music: _____

_____

_____

_____

Drama (optional):   **Actors:** _____

_____

           Props: _____

_____

_____

_____

_____

_____

Closing Prayer: **Read by:** _____

All prayers open with an invitation to God (e.g., God our Father, Lord of Compassion and Goodness, or Gracious God). They continue with words of thanks or praise or humbly ask for God's help. We always make our prayers to God through his Son, Jesus Christ. We end with **Amen**. To complete the prayer service, you may finish with the sign of the cross, the sign of peace, or a closing song.

_____

_____

_____

_____

Amen.

Let us end our prayer service with the sign of the cross: **In the name of the Father, and of the Son, and of the Holy Spirit. Amen.**

If there is a closing song, announce it after the sign of the cross.

Our closing song is: _____

Cantor(s): _____

Instrument(s): _____

CD: _____   Track number: _____

To see the completed Prayer Service at a glance, fill in the **Prayer Service Summary Sheet.**

    These lists are also available for download at www.schools.novalis.ca/SchoolLiturgiesMadeEasy.html

Prayer Service Summary Sheet

(to use on the day of the celebration)

Date of Prayer Service: _____

Title of Prayer Service: _____

Part of the Prayer Service	Song/Reading	Read/Sung by:
Optional: Offerings / Symbols		
Introduction		
Opening Hymn or Song		
Scripture Reading		
Litany (optional)		
Song (optional)		
Prayer of the Faithful (optional)		
Closing Prayer		
Closing Song (optional)		

These lists are also available for download at www.schools.novalis.ca/SchoolLiturgiesMadeEasy.html

Details Checklist

Description	X
Personnel	
Confirm date and time of celebration with priest	
Confirm readers are present	
Confirm altar servers are present (for Masses only)	
Confirm gift bearers are present (for Masses only)	
Confirm that ministers of communion are present (for Masses only)	
Confirm seating	
Designate greeter	
Confirm transportation and equipment set-up	

Description	X
Overview	
Copy of Mass Summary Sheet	
Copy of Prayer Service Summary Sheet	
Readings	
Copies of readings	
Copies of Responsorial Psalm	
Copies of Prayer of the Faithful	
Confirm readers are seated in order	

These lists are also available for download at www.schools.novalis.ca/SchoolLiturgiesMadeEasy.html

Music		Miscellaneous	
Confirm musicians are present		Decoration set-up	
Confirm choir is present		Bible	
Confirm instruments are available		Crucifix	
Confirm cantor is present		Candles	
CD player or mp3 player		Table decorations	
Speakers for mp3 player			
Backup CD (2 copies)		Confirm gifts are in place (for Masses only)	
Copies of music		Stepstool for younger students	
Copies of lyrics		Flashlight	
Overheads			
Overhead machine or laptop		**Other:**	
PowerPoint slides			
Speakers for laptop			
Screen			
Extension cord			
Music stands			
Microphones and sound system			

Appendix 2

Resources – Music

Music for the Parts of the Mass

Note: Choose one Mass setting for all the acclamations of the Eucharistic Prayer.

The 2011 Revised Roman Missal contains some new wording for the Holy, Holy, Holy and the Memorial Acclamation. The Canadian bishops have approved three Mass settings for the revised prayers. All three are found in *Celebrate in Song*. They are by three Canadian composers: Fr. Geoffrey Angeles, John Dawson, and Michel Guimont. You can listen to them on the CCCB website.

Many other well-known Mass settings have been revised as well. These include

"The Mass of Creation," by Marty Haugen

"Mass of Glory," by Ken Canedo and Bob Hurd

"Mass of God's Promise," by Dan Schutte

"Celtic Mass," by Christopher Walker

Search online for more information on these and other Mass settings.

Hymns for School Celebrations

The following list contains familiar hymns and songs organized by theme. The list includes a number of traditional hymns along with hymns from four hymnals that are commonly found in Canadian churches:

• *Gather* (1994) – GIA Publications (ISBN 978-0-94105-057-9)

• *Catholic Book of Worship III* (1994) – Canadian Conference of Catholic Bishops (ISBN 978-0-88997-302-2)

• *Catholic Book of Worship II* (1980) – Canadian Conference of Catholic Bishops (ISBN 0-88997-025-4)

• *Celebrate in Song* (2011) – Canadian Conference of Catholic Bishops (ISBN 979-0-9001411-0-1)

The following resources are specifically for children:

• *Rise Up and Sing* (Young People's Music resource), 2nd edition – Oregon Catholic Press (ISBN 978-1-57992-034-9)

• *Singing Our Faith* (A Hymnal for Young Catholics) – GIA Publications (ISBN 978-1-57999-113-5)

• *Never Too Young* (Spirit and Song for Young People) – Oregon Catholic Press (ISBN 978-1-57992-139-2)

• *Cross Generation (A Hymnal)* – GIA Publications (ISBN 978-1-57999-748-9)

Thanksgiving/Ordinary Time

"Glory and Praise to Our God," by Dan Schutte (*Gather*)

"Here I Am, Lord," by Dan Schutte (*Gather, Catholic Book of Worship [CBW] III*)

"Thank You, Lord" (sung to the tune of "Edelweiss")

"Gather Us In," by Marty Haugen (*Gather, CBW III*)

"We Are Many Parts," by Marty Haugen (*Gather*)

"Shepherd Me, O God," by Marty Haugen (*Gather*)

Remembrance Day

"Prayer of St. Francis" (Make Me a Channel of Your Peace), by Sebastian Temple (*Gather, CBW II*)

"Peace is Flowing Like a River" (*Gather*)

"Let There Be Peace on Earth," by Jill Jackson and Mark Miller

"Sing a New Song," by Dan Schutte (*Gather, CBW III, CBW II*)

"Blest Are They," by David Haas (*Gather, CBW III*)

Advent

"O Come, Divine Messiah" (*CBW III, CBW II*)

"O Come, O Come Emmanuel" (*CBW III, CBW II*)

"Prepare the Way of the Lord" (round), by Jacques Berthier, Taizé community (*CBW III*)

"Like a Shepherd," by Bob Dufford (*Gather, CBW III, CBW II*)

"Soon and Very Soon," by Andrea Crouch (*Gather*)

Lent/ Reconciliation

"The Prodigal Son" (Father, I Have Sinned), by Eugene O'Reilly (*Gather, CBW II*)

"Blest Are They" (*Gather, CBW III*)

"Jesus, Remember Me," by Jacques Berthier, Taizé community (*Gather, CBW III*)

"Jerusalem, My Destiny," by James Moore (*Gather*)

"Come Back to Me" (Hosea), by Gregory Norbert (*Gather, CBW II*)

"Ashes," by Tom Conry (*Gather*)

Easter

"Sing a New Song," by Dan Schutte (*Gather, CBW III, CBW II*)

"Sing to the Mountains," by Bob Dufford (*Gather, CBW II*)

"Jesus Christ is Risen Today," by Charles Wesley (*CBW III, CBW II*)

"Alleluia, Alleluia, Give Thanks to the Risen Lord," by Donald Fishel (*CBW III, CBW II*)

"Join in the Dance," by Dan Schutte (*Celebrate in Song*)

First Communion (for students who have recently celebrated this sacrament in their parish)

"We Come to Your Table," by Mark Daniel Merritt

"Taste and See," by James Moore (*Gather, CBW III, CBW II*)

"His Banner Over Me Is Love"

"One Bread, One Body," by John Foley (*Gather*)

"I Am the Bread of Life," by Suzanne Toolan (*Gather, CBW II*)

"We Come to Your Feast," by Michael Joncas (*Gather*)

"Taste and See," by Michel Guimont (Born of the Spirit Series, Canadian Conference of Catholic Bishops)

Songs about Mary, Mother of God (for Advent)

"Hail Mary, Gentle Woman," by Carey Landry (*Gather*)

"Immaculate Mary" (*CBW III, CBW II*)

Appendix 3

Resources – Books

Core Resources

Directory for Masses with Children
Congregation for Divine Worship (1973)
www.adoremus.org/DMC-73.html

Youth at Worship: A Preparation Guide
Canadian Conference of Catholic Bishops
(1999)
Available from www.cccb.ca

**Masses with Children: Masses
of Reconciliation**
Canadian Catholic Conference (1975)
Available from www.cccb.ca

General Instruction on the Roman Missal
Canadian Conference of Catholic Bishops
(2011)
Available from www.cccb.ca

Constitution on the Sacred Liturgy
Pope Paul VI (1963)
www.vatican.va

Liturgical Calendar / Ordo
Canadian Conference of Catholic Bishops
(published annually)
Available from www.cccb.ca

Prayers and Prayer Services

**Words for the Journey for Kids:
Ten-Minute Prayer Services for Schools**
Lisa Freemantle and Les Miller
(Novalis, 2010)
ISBN 978-2-89646-239-1

**Words for the Journey for Teens:
Ten-Minute Prayer Services for Schools**
Lisa Freemantle, Les Miller and Melinda
Rapallo-Ferrara (Novalis, 2011)
ISBN 978-2-89646-303-9

**Words for the Journey: Ten-Minute Prayer
Services for Teachers and Administrators**
Lisa Freemantle and Les Miller
(Novalis, 2009)
ISBN 978-2-89646-142-4

**Let's Pray! Prayers for
the Elementary Classroom**
Heather Reid (Novalis, 2007)
ISBN 978-2-89507-845-6

My Prayer Book
(Novalis, 2011)
ISBN 978-2-89646-238-4

150 Opening and Closing Prayers
Carl Koch (Saint Mary's Press, 2001)
ISBN 0-88489-241-7

Masses with Students

Masses with Young People
Donal Neary, SJ
(Twenty-Third Publications, 1987)
ISBN 0-89622-295-0

50 Children's Liturgies for all Occasions
Francesca Kelly
(Twenty-Third Publications, 1995)
ISBN 0-89622-541-0

The Complete Children's Liturgy Book: Liturgies of the Word for Years A B C
Katie Thompson (Twenty-Third Publications, 1995)
ISBN 0-89622-6956

Lectionary for Masses with Children
Liturgical Press (1991)
ISBN 0-8146-6139-4

SUNDAY Lectionary for Children,
Years A, B and C
(Novalis, 1989)

Sunday Missal
(Novalis: published annually)

Sunday Missal for Young Catholics
(Novalis: published annually)

Children's Lectionary
John Behnke (Paulist Press, 1974)
ISBN 978-0-8091-1857-1

Where to Find Things in the Bible

The Catholic Bible Concordance for the New Revised Standard Version – Catholic Edition
C.W. Lyons and Thomas Deliduka
(The Catholic Company, 2009)
978-1931018494

Where to Find It in the Bible
Ken Anderson
(Thomas Nelson Publishers, 1996)
ISBN 0-7852-1157-8

Liturgical Dance

Liturgical Dance: A Practical Guide to Dancing in Worship
Deena Bess Sherman (Express Press, 2004)
ISBN 978-0788021237

Praise Him in the Dance
Regina S. Wright (Author House, 2005)
ISBN 978-1-4208-0462-1

More Resources for Elementary Schools

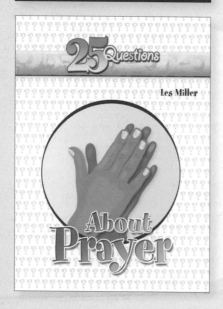

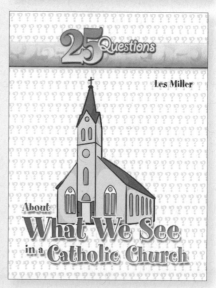